Rev It Up!

DRAGSTERS

by Thomas K. Adamson

Consulting Editor: Gail Saunders-Smith, PhD

Consultant: Leslie Kendall, Curator
Petersen Automotive Museum, Los Angeles

CAPSTONE PRESS
a capstone imprint

Pebble Plus is published by Capstone Press,
151 Good Counsel Drive, P.O. Box 669, Mankato, Minnesota 56002.
www.capstonepub.com

Library of Congress Cataloging-in-Publication Data
Adamson, Thomas K., 1970–
  Dragsters / by Thomas K. Adamson.
    p. cm.—(Pebble plus. Rev it up!)
  Includes bibliographical references and index.
  Summary: "Simple text and full-color photographs briefly describe the history and unique features of dragsters"—
Provided by publisher.
  ISBN 978-1-4296-5319-0 (library binding)
  1. Dragsters—Juvenile literature. I. Title. II. Series.
  TL236.2.A33 2011
  629.228—dc22
                                                                    2010025022

Editorial Credits
Erika L. Shores, editor; Ted Williams, designer; Laura Manthe, production specialist

Photo Credits
Auto Imagery, Inc., cover, 1, 5, 7, 9, 13, 15, 17, 19, 21
Getty Images Inc. /Workbook Stock/Matthew Wakem, 11

Artistic Effects
Shutterstock/Alexander Chaikin, argus, dedaiva bg, jeffreychin

Note to Parents and Teachers

The Rev It Up! series supports national social studies standards related to science, technology,
and society. This book describes and illustrates dragsters. The images support early readers
in understanding the text. The repetition of words and phrases helps early readers learn new
words. This book also introduces early readers to subject-specific vocabulary words, which are
defined in the Glossary section. Early readers may need assistance to read some words and to
use the Table of Contents, Glossary, Read More, Internet Sites, and Index sections of the book.

Printed in the United States of America in North Mankato, Minnesota.

092010   005933CGS11

Table of Contents

Super Speed 4

Dragster History 10

Parts of a Dragster 14

Rev It Up! 20

Glossary 22

Read More 23

Internet Sites 23

Index 24

Super Speed

Dragsters are the quickest cars in the world. Zoooom! They roar down the track at more than 300 miles (483 kilometers) per hour.

Dragsters race on a short, straight track called a drag strip. Drag strips can be ¼ mile (0.4 km) or ⅛ mile (0.2 km) long.

A row of lights lets drivers

know when to start

the drag race. The lights

are called a Christmas tree.

Vroom! Green means go!

Dragster History

People used to drag race
on streets. They added
parts to their cars
to make them faster.
Street races were dangerous.

In 1951, the National Hot Rod Association formed. It makes rules to keep drag racing safe. But the racing is still fast and fun.

13

Parts of a Dragster

Dragsters have huge rear tires.

The smooth tires are

called slicks.

They grip the track.

Airfoils help drivers control

the dragster at high speeds.

An airfoil causes air

to push the dragster's tires

down on the track.

airfoil

airfoil

17

Brakes alone won't stop
a dragster. Poof!
Parachutes help it
slow down.

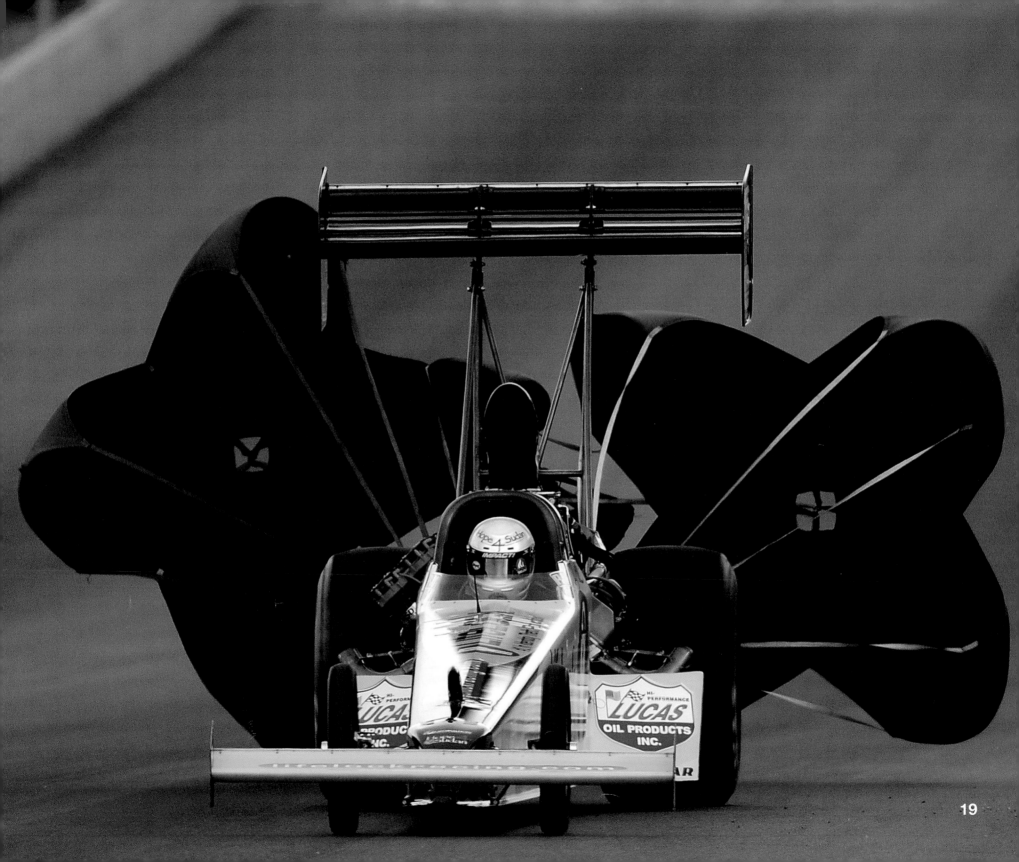

Rev It Up!

A drag race lasts only
about five seconds.
But dragsters pack a lot
of speed into a short race.

Glossary

airfoil—a winglike feature attached to a dragster

drag race—a race in which two cars begin at a standstill and drive in a straight line at high speeds for a short distance

drag strip—the short, straight track dragsters race on

parachute—a large piece of strong fabric; the parachute flies out behind a dragster at the end of the race to help slow down the car

slick—a racing tire made with a smooth, soft surface that more easily grips the track

Read More

Poolos, J. *Wild About Dragsters*. Wild Rides. New York: PowerKids Press, 2008.

Von Finn, Denny. *Top Fuel Dragsters*. Torque: The World's Fastest. Minneapolis: Bellwether Media, 2010.

Zuehlke, Jeffrey. *Drag Racers*. Motor Mania. Minneapolis: Lerner, 2008.

Internet Sites

FactHound offers a safe, fun way to find Internet sites related to this book. All of the sites on FactHound have been researched by our staff.

Here's all you do:

Visit *www.facthound.com*

Type in this code: 9781429653190

Super-cool stuff! Check out projects, games and lots more at **www.capstonekids.com**

Index

airfoils, 16

brakes, 18

Christmas tree, 8

lights, 8

National Hot Rod
    Association, 12

parachutes, 18

rules, 12

slicks, 14

speed, 4, 16, 20

street racing, 10

tires, 14, 16

tracks, 4, 6, 14, 16

Word Count: 185
Grade: 1
Early-Intervention Level: 18